To Linda
with love
Lorna

I AM BECOMING MY MOTHER

I AM BECOMING MY MOTHER

Lorna Goodison

New Beacon Books
London – Port of Spain

First published 1986
by New Beacon Books Ltd.,
76 Stroud Green Road, London N4 3EN, England.

© 1986 Lorna Goodison

All rights reserved. No part of this book may be reproduced in any form or by any means without prior written permission of the Publisher, excepting brief quotes used in connection with reviews written specifically for inclusion in a magazine or newspaper.

ISBN 0901241 67 9 hardback
0901241 68 7 paperback

Printed by Villiers Publications Ltd.,
26a Shepherds Hill, London N6 5AH, England.

Dedicated
to my son Miles
to the Big Women of Harvey River
Dorice, Ann, Rose, Barbara, Betty,
Joan and Anya — and in memory of
Jo, Nanie and Joyce Bending.

ACKNOWLEDGEMENTS
Special thanks to Professor Edward Baugh and to Creation For Liberation (London).

CONTENTS

My Last Poem	7
Mulatta Song	9
Jamaica 1980	10
Bend-Down Plaza	11
We Are The Women	12
Garden Of The Women Once Fallen	14
Dream — August 1979	16
Songs For My Son	17
My Will	19
Homecoming	21
Caravanserai	22
Mulatta Song II	24
The Mulatta As Penelope	25
Farewell Our Trilogy	26
Tightrope Walker	27
Lepidopterist	29
On Becoming A Mermaid	30
The Mulatta And The Minotaur	31
'Mine O Thou Lord Of Life, Send My Roots Rain'	32
Keith Jarrett — Rainmaker	33
Invoke Mercy Extraordinary For Angels Fallen	34
Jah Music	36
Lullaby For Jean Rhys	37
I Am Becoming My Mother	38
Guinea Woman	39
For Rosa Parks	41
Bedspread	42
Nanny	44
For My Mother (May I Inherit Half Her Strength)	46
Letters To The Egyptian	49

MY LAST POEM

I once wrote poems
that emerged so fine
with a rough edge for honing
a soft cloth for polishing
and a houseproud eye
I'd pride myself in making them shine.
But in this false winter
with the real cold to come
no, this season's shift
there are no winters here,
well call it what you will but the cold time is here
with its memorial crosses to mark
my father's dying
and me wondering where next year will find me
in whose vineyard toiling,
I gave my son
to a kind woman to keep
and walked down through the valley
on my scarred feet,
across the river
and into the guilty town
in search of bread
but they had closed the bakery down,
so I returned and said child
there was no bread
I'll write you my last poem instead
my last poem is not my best
all things weaken towards the end.
O but it should be laid out
and chronicled, crazy like my life
with a place for all my several lives
daughter, sister, mistress, friend, warrior
wife
and a high holy ending for the blessed
one
me as mother to a man.
There should be a place for
messages and replies

you are too tightly bound, too whole
he said
I loosened my hair and I bled
now you send conflicting signals they said
divided I turned both ways and fled.
There should be a place for all this
but I'm almost at the end of my last poem
and I'm almost a full woman.
I warm my son's clothes
in this cold time
in the deep of my bosom
and I'm not afraid of love.
In fact, should it be
that these are false signals I'm receiving
and not a real unqualified ending
I'm going to keep the word love
and use it in my next poem.
I know it's just the wordsmith's failing
to forge a new metal to ring like its rhyme
but I'll keep its fool's gold
for you see it's always bought me time.
And if I write another poem
I'm going to use it
for it has always used me
and if I ever write another poem
I'm going to return that courtesy.

MULATTA SONG

Very well Mulatta,
this dance must end.
This half-arsed band
blowing its own
self-centered song.
The bass slack stringed
slapped by some wall-eyed
mother's son.
This session must done
soon done.
O how you danced Mulatta
to the music in your head
pretending that their notes
were your notes.
Till the gateman whispered
into the side of your head
'Mulatta, mulatta, that's the
dance of the dead'.
So you rubadub and rentatile
and hustle a little
smiling the while
pretending that
this terrible din
is a well tuned air
on a mandolin.
And Mulatta your red dress
you wore here as new
is a wet hibiscus
what will you do?
Fold the petals of the skirt
and sit this last long
last song out.
Bind up the blood-wound
from the heart on your sleeve
And now Mulatta it's time to leave.

JAMAICA 1980

It trails always behind me
a webbed seine with a catch of fantasy
a penance I pay for being me
who took the order of poetry.
Always there with the gaping holes
and the mended ones, and the stand-in words.
But this time my Jamaica
my green-clad muse
this time your callings are of no use
I am spied on by your mountains
wire-tapped by your secret streams
your trees dripping blood-leaves
and jasmine selling tourist-dreams.

For over all this edenism
hangs the smell of necromancy
and each man eats his brother's flesh
Lord, so much of the cannibal left
in the jungle on my people's tongues.

We've sacrificed babies
and burnt our mothers
as payment to some viridian-eyed God dread
who works in cocaine under hungry men's heads.

And mine the task of writing it down
as I ride in shame round this blood-stained town.
And when the poem refuses to believe
and slimes to aloes in my hands
mine is the task of burying the dead
I the late madonna of barren lands.

BEND-DOWN PLAZA

The whole place is a market place
those inside selling
what dem outside higglering
only outside you might get it for less
if you beat down the money-till
stored in her breasts.

Outside the temples of very
graciousness living
guardy guards with a dobermann's aid
a dog trained to bite to the bones
guardy well-trash in a pipe-up uniform
a sleeping form
'Dem shoulda give the dog the uniform'
but guardy just a sleep and a dream
bout a fine fat girl in a furrwhosee jeans.
'So whappen if black people can't
advertise dem
Nobody no want see them, dem must
only buy them.'
And the dog throttles low
at the sharp-green smell of a passing
negro.

Bend down nice lady
bend down
but try not to bend too deep
for Jah inna this plaza
distributing diseases
and it look like God a sleep.

WE ARE THE WOMEN

We are the women
with thread bags
anchored deep in our bosoms
containing blood agreements
silver coins and cloves of garlic
and an apocrypha
of Nanny's secrets.

We've made peace
with want
if it doesn't kill us
we'll live with it.

We ignore promises
of plenty
we know that old sankey.

We are the ones
who are always waiting
mouth corner white
by sepulchres and
bone yards
for the bodies of our men,
waiting under massa
waiting under massa table
for the trickle down of crumbs.

We are the women
who ban our bellies
with strips from the full moon
our nerves made keen
from hard grieving
worn thin like
silver sixpences.

We've buried our hope
too long
as the anchor to our
navel strings
we are rooting at
the burying spot
we are uncovering
our hope.

GARDEN OF THE WOMEN ONCE FALLEN

I

SHAME MI LADY

Lady, what could you have done so
to make you close in on yourself so?

The lady folds her arms across her chest
The lady droops her head between her breasts.

The lady's eyes will not answer yours.
Lady, if I tell you my crime
will you tell me yours?

Mine are legion and all to do with love misplaced
yet I've been replanted in this arboreal place,
now, if I can find favour (me with my bold face)
you bashful you shy you innocent lady
must/bound to find absolution/grace.

Come lady, tie bright ribbon-grass round your waist
Let you and I bloom redemption in this place.

II

BROOM WEED

You exhaust yourself so
O weed powerless
your life devoted to sweeping, cleaning
even in your fullest blooming.
You pull dust balls from the air
whisk away bee-droppings
with your coarsened hair.
And in your fullness
they bundle you
without so much
as a by-your-leave.
Drudges, make a coat of arms
wear broomweed on your sleeves.

III

POUI

She don't put out for just anyone.
She waits for HIM
and in his high august heat
he takes her
and their celestial mating
is so intense
that for weeks her rose-gold dress
lies tangled round her feet
and she don't even notice.

IV

SUNFLOWER POSSESSED

Her folded neck-skin
reveals her age
but the face powdered
is limned by myriads
of mirrors and gold-washed frills.
This display is for the benefit
of the perfect one in the sky.
To the ragged coterie of weeds round her
she says, 'In my first bloom I was
the tender honey-skinned mamma
of that great golden one on high'.
The ragged weeds
never knowing glory
(for this reason some weeds are evil)
shiver their rags and hiss
'sure'
she semaphores, hoping
the golden circle of her unmaking
will give her the go round once more.

DREAM — AUGUST 1979

The sacrificial pigeon clears the roof.
The sun strikes,
his heart sprouts a hibiscus
glowing primary red
he too has joined the feathered ranks of the dead.
On Mount Zion the obeah man balms
on the battlefield below we with
bloodied hands
sight-read psalms.
The deed is done, the chosen have won.
And over Mount Rosser a wash-line flags
squares in birds-eye say there is a babe within
Only the bush promises healing.

SONGS FOR MY SON

I

My son cries
the cats answer
I hover over his sleeping
suspended on his milk-stained breath
I live in fear of his hurt, his death.
The fear is real
if I close my eyes when it is at its height
I see him curled man-in-miniature asleep.
I hover over his milk-stained breath
and listen for its rise
every one an assurance that he is alive
and if God bargains
I strike a deal with him,
for his life I owe you something, anything
but please let no harm come to him.
The cat cries
my son answers
his sleep is short
his stomach hurts.

II

They gather from beyond
through the trees they come
gather on the banks of the family river
one by one they raise the keening song
great grandmother Rebecca of the healing hands
Tata Edward, Bucky, and Brownman
my father's lost mother Maria
and now my father
come to sing the birthsong
and Hannah horsewoman to ride me through.

It's a son, a great grand grandson, a man
born to a headstrong, heartfoolish woman,
part the birth waters with river-washed hands
and let the newson through,
woman born of strong-limbed woman
woman born to parents in peacetime
behold your son
flesh of your flesh
your life's work begun.

III

The midwife
tie-head African woman
fingers like healing-roots
feeds me thyme-tea
to hurry on your coming
summons the appropriate spirits
to witness your crowning,
a knife keen with garlic
to sever you from me
and we'll never smell
its primal top-notes
you or I
without memories of our joining.

IV

I'll name you Miles I say
for the music, and for coming
a long way
you suck, my womb pulls
the thirst constant
the connection three-way.

MY WILL

Son, my will,
albeit premature
when the palm readers
divine
for me an extended
life line.

Besides who knows what
worth bequeathing
I could acquire
before the life line
inches to the darker side
of my hand.

But, for a start,
the gift of song,
this sweet immediate source
of release was not given me
so I leave it for you in the hope
that God takes hints.
Then the right to call
all older than you
Miss, mister or mistress
in the layered love of our
simplest ways,
eat each day's salt and bread
with praise,
and may you never know hungry.
And books
I mean the love of them.

May you like me earn good
friends
but just to be sure,
love books.
When bindings fall apart
they can be fixed
you will find

that is not always so
with friendships.
And no gold.
Too many die/kill for it
besides its face is too bold.
This observation is the
last I give :
most times assume a
patina a shade subdued
so when you bloom they
will value it.

HOMECOMING

From the east window
Touchau, story-teller
speaks tales of homecoming
concerning my warrior.
So I've made my bed
a plateau.
Outside euphorbia flurries snow
allamanda and poinsettia
shout down a false winter
into silence
for the coming of my warrior.

CARAVANSERAI

Elliptical moon
rims the yellow/brown
woman
dream seller.
Brass basins of blood
brass basins of wine
a pebbled hour glass
to texture time.

She dyes her palms
and divines on sand.
The moon bellied-out
stirs the tides' motion
within
the infant heads down
for the beginning.
The tide water breaks
the motion stays her hand.

And did you see
that quiet caravan
with muffled bells
and no colours to speak of
except the face
ebony/indigo
of the young camel driver
dream buyer?

He spoke to her of nights
by the Nile,
said there was Egypt
in her hair
and watered down
at the caravanserai there.

The woman
bends to deliver
by a tributary
of the Euphrates river
where lions drink
and an occasional hyena.
Brass basins of blood
brass basins of water.

MULATTA SONG - II

Mulatta of the loose-sieved hands
frail madonna of bloodstained lands

    Yes I am the lady
    this is the right door
    the house covered in green
    the red lantern
    the grey and white cats
    and the secrets
    in the sandalwood box.
    You've come seeking
    a poem you say
    and somebody directed you
    this way?
    Yes this is the house
    of the lady poet
    she wears black and heavy silver
    there is calm within
    when evening comes
    she offers you wine
    and sometimes her smile
    and sometimes herself
    but mostly she sits
    and sings to herself.

THE MULATTA AS PENELOPE

Tonight I'll pull your limbs through small
soft garments
Your head will part my breasts
and you will hear a different heartbeat.
Today we said the real goodbye, he and I
but this time
I will not sit and spin and spin
the door open to let the madness in
till the sailor finally weary
of the sea
returns with tin souvenirs and a claim
to me.
True, I returned from the quayside
my eyes full of sand
and his salt leaving smell
fresh on my hands
But, you're my anchor awhile now
and that goes deep,
I'll sit in the sun and dry my hair
while you sleep.

FAREWELL OUR TRILOGY

No, love, there are no new poems
not since the monsoon of six months or so.
Once or twice I've felt what I thought
was water breaking three days running
but it turned out to be playbacks from
your leaving. The only news
is that some time on Sunday
a boy from the village above here
said he saw Sheba-cat in the dry-river bed
her throat stained, her long legs stiffened
in death, and, yes, as always
she had been quick with kittens.
But she's laid her down on the cool river stones
and exchanged her ninth life for
peace deep to the bones
and I'm writing this finally to say
that our cat was the last proof
that you and I mated
and raised up houses with the pillars
of our great love that corroded into hatred
and on Monday it rained hard
enough to bear her out to sea.
In this place I'm all that remains
of our trilogy.

TIGHTROPE WALKER

And I have been a tightrope walker all my life,
that is, tightrope walking has been my main occupation.
In between stints in sundry fraudulent circuses
I've worked at poetry, making pictures
or being a paid smart-arse.
Once I even tried my hand at cashiering,
couldn't balance the ledger though
but I was honest, always overpaid someone
and had to make up the shortfall myself.
But it was too firm on the ground
so I put on my fishnet tights
my irridiscent kingfisher blue bathing-suit
chalked the soles of my slippers of pliable gold kid
and took to the ropes again.

It's a fine life, those uncontained moments
in the air
those nerve-stretched belly-bottom spasms
from here to there
and your receiver copping what
from the ground looks like
an innocent feel
as he steadies you safely on the far side.
But I broke both arms
and the side of my head once
and had multiple miscarriages from
falling flat on my back
so I'm on the ground most days now
except for this, the tightest walk of all.
I don my new costume of
marabou and flamingo feathers
and my shade of oyster juliet cap
with the discreet spangles
and inch toward you once or twice a week.
I have to make record time
you have to be home before dark
and the entire act is really a rehearsal
here in this empty tent with last night's

sawdust to buffer the wild in our talk
and the fat lady sunning herself outside
and listening for secrets in our laughter
and it's all done with safety nets, thank you
and no audience invited to the finest
performances of me and you
but it's my life and my last act
before our show closes down
and re-opens to a gaping public
at some other circus ground.

LEPIDOPTERIST

'I've done my best to immortalise what I failed to keep.'
— Joseph Brodsky

And now I am a lepidopterist
with my rows of bitter pins
securing here, now there
the flown species wings.
If we soak the memories
in our bile
they will keep and crystallise
come clear
in the heat of this now poisoned air.
I thought I had you/where are you?
You gave up on us/I gave up on you
You changed your mind/I'm changing mine
Lord, even in death the wings beat so.
Hold still
let me put this last row in.

ON BECOMING A MERMAID

Watching the underlife idle by
you think drowning must be easy death
just let go and let the water carry you
away and under
the current pulls your bathing-plaits loose
your hair floats out straightened by the water
your legs close together fuse all the length down
your feet now one broad foot
the toes spread into
a fish-tail, fan-like
your sex locked under
mother-of-pearl scales
you're a nixie now, a mermaid
a green tinged fish/fleshed woman/thing
who swims with thrashing movements
and stands upended on the sea floor
breasts full and floating buoyed by the salt
and the space between your arms now always
filled and your sex sealed forever under
mother-of-pearl scale/locks closes finally
on itself like some close-mouthed oyster.

THE MULATTA AND THE MINOTAUR

And shall I tell you what the minotaur said to me
as we dined by the Nile on almond eyes and tea?
No, I shall not reveal that yet.
Here, I'll record just how we met.
We faced each other and a bystander said,
'Shield your eyes, he's wearing God's head'
but it was already turbulent and deeply stained
with the merciless indigo of hell's rain.
And I, delaying my dying, hung my innocence high
and it glowed pale and waterwash against the sky.
And we met, but he was on his way
So he marked my left breast with this stain
which is indelible till we meet again.
And our lives rocketed through separate centuries
and we gave life to sons in sevens
and I was suckled of a great love or two
split not all the way asunder
and stuck together with glue.
And he wed the faultless wind
and wrestled with phantasms
and fantastic djinn
and came through the other side whole and alone
with a countenance clear as wind-worried bones
and the seal of a serpent engorged by a dove
imprinted on marching orders for love.
And I was suckled of a great love or two
split not all the way asunder
and stuck together with glue.
For the Queen of Sheba had willed me
her bloodstone ring,
a flight of phoenix feathers
and her looser black things.
So,
Minotaur;
God's-head wearer
Galileo
Conqueror-of-Paris
Someone I don't know
There will be a next time
Centuries ago.

'MINE, O THOU LORD OF LIFE, SEND MY ROOTS RAIN'

— Gerard Manley Hopkins

For I've been planted long
in a sere dry place
watered only occasionally
with odd overflows
from a passing cloud's face.
In my morning
I imitated the bougainvillea
(in appearances
I'm hybrid)
I gave forth defiant alleluias
of flowering
covered my aridity with
red petalled blisters
grouped close, from far
they were a borealis of
save-face flowers.
In the middle of my
life span
my trunk's not so limber
my sap flows thicker
my region has posted signs
that speak of scarce water.
At night God, I feel
my feet powder.
Lord let the preying worms
wait to feast in vain.
In this noon of my orchard
send me deep rain.

KEITH JARRETT — RAINMAKER

Piano man
my roots are african
I dwell in the centre of the sun.
I am used to its warmth
I am used to its heat
I am seared by its vengeance
(it has a vengeful streak)

So my prayers are usually
for rain.
My people are farmers
and artists
and sometimes the lines
blur
so a painting becomes a
december of sorrel
a carving heaps like a yam hill
or a song of redemption wings
like the petals of resurrection
lilies — all these require rain.
So this sunday
when my walk misses
my son's balance on my hips
I'll be alright if you pull down
for me
waterfalls of rain.
I never thought a piano
could divine
but I'm hearing you this morning
and right on time
its drizzling now
I'll open the curtains and
watch the lightning conduct
your hands.

INVOKE MERCY EXTRAORDINARY FOR ANGELS FALLEN

In his 30th year
in search of signs
God's face appeared to him
on the surface of a brackish pond
littered with leaves
The face of God
was so suffused with light
light so intense
that the rotting leaves
were cremated
and the salt sullen water
rose clear.

Thereafter he would say,
The face of God
can not be described
but l am grateful
I was kneeling.
And the man kneeling
and the man kneeling
heard in his head
a mighty keening

Who knows what God
in his speaking
said to the man kneeling
but messages lodged in his lungs
were released
as a clean new source of singing.

What else is there
for the eyes to hold in wonder
after they have framed
the face of God?

He spent a lifetime after
alchemising the visage
from pain and white powder.

Invoke mercy extraordinary
for angels fallen
Father,
hasten the end.

JAH MUSIC

(For Michael Cooper)

The sound bubbled up
through a cistern one night
and piped its way into
the atmosphere
and decent people wanted
to know
'What kind of ole nayga music is that
playing on the Government's radio?'
But this red and yellow and dark green
sound
stained from travelling underground
smelling of poor people's dinners
from a yard dense as Belgium
has the healing
more than weed and white rum healing
more than bush tea and fever grass cooling
and it pulses without a symphony conductor
all it need is a dub organiser.

LULLABY FOR JEAN RHYS

SLEEP IT OFF LADY
the night nurse is here
dressed in rain forest colours
used stars in her hair.
Drink this final dark potion
and straighten your night-dress
wear your transparent slippers
you must look your best
for you just might go dancing
atop hard-headed trees
with a man who is virile
and anxious to please.

Sleep now Miss Rhys.

I AM BECOMING MY MOTHER

Yellow/brown woman
fingers smelling always of onions

My mother raises rare blooms
and waters them with tea
her birth waters sang like rivers
my mother is now me

My mother had a linen dress
the colour of the sky
and stored lace and damask
tablecloths
to pull shame out of her eye.

I am becoming my mother
brown/yellow woman
fingers smelling always of onions.

GUINEA WOMAN

Great grandmother
was a guinea woman
wide eyes turning
the corners of her face
could see behind her
her cheeks dusted with
a fine rash of jet-bead warts
that itched when the rain set up.

Great grandmother's waistline
the span of a headman's hand
slender and tall like a cane stalk
with a guinea woman's antelope-quick walk
and when she paused
her gaze would look to sea
her profile fine like some obverse impression
on a guinea coin from royal memory.

It seems her fate was anchored
in the unfathomable sea
for great grandmother caught the eye of a sailor
whose ship sailed without him from Lucea harbour.
Great grandmother's royal scent of
cinnamon and escallions
drew the sailor up the straits of Africa,
the evidence my blue-eyed grandmother
the first Mulatta
taken into backra's household
and covered with his name.
They forbade great grandmother's
guinea woman presence
they washed away her scent of
cinnamon and escallions
controlled the child's antelope walk
and called her uprisings rebellions.

But, great grandmother
I see your features blood dark
appearing
in the children of each new
breeding
the high yellow brown
is darkening down.
Listen, children
it's great grandmother's turn.

FOR ROSA PARKS

And how was this soft-voiced woman to know
that this 'No'
in answer to the command to rise
would signal the beginning
of the time of walking?
Soft the word
like the closing of some aweful book
a too-long story
with no pauses for reason
but yes, an ending
and the signal to begin the walking.
But the people had walked before
in yoked formations down to Calabar
into the belly of close-ribbed whales
sealed for seasons
and unloaded to walk again
alongside cane stalks tall as men.
No, walking was not new to them.
Saw a woman tie rags to her feet
running red, burnishing the pavements,
a man with no forty acres
just a mule
riding towards Jerusalem
And the children small somnambulists
moving in the before day morning
And the woman who never raised her voice
never lowered her eyes
just kept walking
leading us towards sunrise.

BEDSPREAD

Sometimes in the still
unchanging afternoons
when the memories crowded
hot and hopeless against
her brow
she would seek its cool colours
and signal him to lie down
in his cell.
It is three in the afternoon Nelson
let us rest here together
upon this bank draped in freedom
colour.
It was woven by women with slender
capable hands
accustomed to binding wounds
hands that closed the eyes of
dead children,
that fought for the right to
speak in their own tongues
in their own land
in their own schools.
They wove the bedspread
and knotted notes of hope
in each strand
and selvedged the edges with
ancient blessings
older than any white man's coming.
So in the afternoons lying on this
bright bank of blessing
Nelson my husband I meet you in dreams
my beloved much of the world too is
asleep blind to the tyranny and evil
devouring our people.
But, Mandela, you are rock on this sand
harder than any metal
mined in the bowels of this land
you are purer than any
gold tempered by fire

shall we lie here wrapped
in the colours of our free Azania?
They arrested the bedspread.
They and their friends are working
to arrest the dreams in our heads
and the women, accustomed to closing
the eyes of the dead
are weaving cloths still brighter
to drape us in glory in a Free
Azania.

NANNY

My womb was sealed
with molten wax
of killer bees
for nothing should enter
nothing should leave
the state of perpetual siege
the condition of the warrior.

From then my whole body would quicken
at the birth of everyone of my people's children.
I was schooled in the green-giving ways
of the roots and vines
made accomplice to the healing acts
of Chainey root, fever grass & vervain.

My breasts flattened
settled unmoving against my chest
my movements ran equal
to the rhythms of the forest.

I could sense and sift
the footfall of men
from the animals
and smell danger
death's odour
in the wind's shift.

When my eyes rendered
light from the dark
my battle song opened
into a solitaire's moan
I became most knowing
and forever alone.

And when my training was over
they circled my waist with pumpkin seeds
and dried okra, a traveller's jigida
and sold me to the traders
all my weapons within me.
I was sent, tell that to history.

When your sorrow obscures the skies
other women like me will rise.

FOR MY MOTHER (MAY I INHERIT HALF HER STRENGTH)

My mother loved my father
I write this as an absolute
in this my thirtieth year
the year to discard absolutes

he appeared, her fate disguised,
as a sunday player in a cricket match,
he had ridden from a country
one hundred miles south of hers.

She tells me he dressed the part,
visiting dandy, maroon blazer
cream serge pants, seam like razor,
and the beret and the two-tone shoes.

My father stopped to speak to her sister,
till he looked and saw her by the oleander,
sure in the kingdom of my blue-eyed grandmother.
He never played the cricket match that day.

He wooed her with words and he won her.
He had nothing but words to woo her,
On a visit to distant Kingston he wrote,

'I stood on the corner of King Street and looked,
and not one woman in that town was lovely as you'.

My mother was a child of the petite bourgeoisie
studying to be a teacher, she oiled her hands
to hold pens.
My father barely knew his father, his mother died young,
he was a boy who grew with his granny.

My mother's trousseau came by steamer through the snows
of Montreal
where her sisters Albertha of the cheekbones and the

perennial Rose, combed Jewlit backstreets with French-
turned names for Doris' wedding things.

Such a wedding Harvey River, Hanover, had never seen
Who anywhere had seen a veil fifteen chantilly yards long?
and a crepe de chine dress with inlets of silk godettes
and a neck-line clasped with jewelled pins!

And on her wedding day she wept. For it was a brazen bride
                                                                          in those days
who smiled.
and her bouquet looked for the world like a sheaf of wheat
against the unknown of her belly,
a sheaf of wheat backed by maidenhair fern, representing Harvey
                                                                                           River
her face washed by something other than river water.

My father made one assertive move, he took the imported
                                                                          cherub down
from the heights of the cake and dropped it in the soft territory
between her breasts . . . and she cried.

When I came to know my mother many years later, I knew her
                                                                        as the figure
who sat at the first thing I learned to read : 'SINGER', and
                                                                     she breast-fed
my brother while she sewed; and she taught us to read while
                                                                     she sewed and
she sat in judgement over all our disputes as she sewed.

She could work miracles, she would make a garment from a
                                                                   square of cloth
in a span that defied time. Or feed twenty people on a
                                                                      stew made from
fallen-from-the-head cabbage leaves and a carrot and a
                                                                  cho-cho and a palmful
of meat.

And she rose early and sent us clean into the world and she
                                                          went to bed in
the dark, for my father came in always last.

There is a place somewhere where my mother never took the
                                                           younger ones
a country where my father with the always smile
my father whom all women loved, who had the perpetual quality
                                                                 of wonder
given only to a child . . . hurt his bride.

Even at his death there was this 'Friend' who stood by her side,
but my mother is adamant that that has no place in the memory
                                                                        of
my father.

When he died, she sewed dark dresses for the women amongst us
and she summoned that walk, straight-backed, that she gave
                                                                             to us
and buried him dry-eyed.

Just that morning, weeks after
she stood delivering bananas from their skin
singing in that flat hill country voice

she fell down a note to the realization that she did
not have to be brave, just this once
and she cried.

For her hands grown coarse with raising nine children
for her body for twenty years permanently fat
for the time she pawned her machine for my sister's
Senior Cambridge fees
and for the pain she bore with the eyes of a queen

and she cried also because she loved him.

LETTERS TO THE EGYPTIAN

1

In case you do not recognise me
when I arrive at Alexandria
I will be wearing a long loose
jade green dress
My hair will be hidden
under a striped fringed headscarf
and I will smell of roseapples and musk.
O love, forgive my vanity,
it is also to make sure
you recognise me
five pounds lighter
drawn from the long journey.
I will bring you a garland
of search-mi-heart leaves
on their underside
I've sewn some woman's tongue seeds
You said you loved my chatter.

2

When the longboat
drew into Khartoum
where the White Nile meets the Blue
I was tempted to abandon ship.
You see there was this Kushite once
who . . .
But how could he ever
compare to you?
I settled instead for buying
at a bazaar Sheba's silver earrings
facsimiles of tiny steeds they are
sprouting forged feathered wings
for you I found a brass horse
one hand high
you can ride across a table's distance,

some sweet salve for easing knots
in shoulders
and a purchase now private
till we're alone and unveil it.
O how could I have thought of
the Kushite —
And am I now nearer to you?
Does the Nile hold all the world's water?
How far is Khartoum from you?

3

Last night there was such
a storm at sea
I sought level
and chained myself with prayers.
(They held)
and in the after
in the soughing of the wind
I'm sure it was you
I heard sing,
Sleep now beloved
fold yourself in softened sails
I wait for you in the Aftergale.
Calm will be our mooring.